# ORIGINAL BODIES

Winner of the 2013 Michael Waters Poetry Prize

Published by the University of Southern Indiana
Evansville, Indiana

ISBN 978-1-930508-30-9   First Edition
Printed in the USA

This publication is made possible by the support of the Indiana Arts Commission, the National Endowment for the Arts, the Vanderburgh Community Foundation, the University of Southern Indiana College of Liberal Arts, the USI Foundation, and the USI Society for Arts & Humanities.

*Southern Indiana Review* Press
Orr Center #2009
University of Southern Indiana
8600 University Boulevard
Evansville, Indiana 47712

sir@usi.edu
*www.southernindianareview.org*

Library of Congress Control Number: 2014944179

Cover art: *Cosmic Bodies* by Sarah Nguyen; *www.sanguyen.com*
Cover design: Sarah Nguyen and Zach Weigand

*For Beth and Lee*

# Contents

# CROW

# TONGUE

*We find human faces in the moon, armies in the clouds...*

—David Hume

# CROW, MOON, CROW

So here is how I remember it:
*a child is a crow is a moon is a river.*
Everything multiplying after midnight
as in a dream: *one crow, two crows, three crows.*
And from the tracks where we look down
at the scooped burrow of the river,
curled this June like a discarded snake skin,
there is a moon growing its canker
on the ridge's shoulder. And up ahead,
in the wet woods, the smell. No garden here
but dead leaves. An augury of matted loam
clinging to boot bottoms. But not even that.
Or say we imagine pale green shoots
that might be fairy wands or spiderworts
or wingstems. Which is another way of saying
we are bound to the earth. Imagine
the sucking sounds of our boots cleaving
to the mud. For here is how I remember it:
*a river is a moon is a crow is a tongue.*

*RIVER*

# LIFE IN THE WOODS

In my uncle's diary of symptoms, light
is described as washed-out moon.
Color as winter fields: gray sky, gray earth.
Shapes forming of their own volition,
strange geometries of line, lacquered splotches
coalescing then disappearing. He blamed
decades of wind, dust kicking up, grit catching
and congealing—or witnessing a younger
brother dying slowly from metastatic brain tumors.
Eventually the pages of the diary dissolved
for him into dark hallways, so I transcribed
the symptoms for the doctor, a task that reminded
me of high school when I copied out long passages
from *Walden*: whip-poor-wills chanting their vespers,
fluviatile trees, the ceaseless roar and pelting
of rainstorms. At sixteen I gave my lone copy—
spine fissured, pages bent back and loose from
their moorings—to a girl I hoped would understand,
but she returned the book in less
than an hour to say, *I wouldn't ever live like that*.
Which I recalled the August morning I arrived
at my uncle's farm to find him on his front porch,
a compendium of jays calling from the willows
by the wire fence. The old man was sitting on a lawn
chair with nothing but his quietude, his face dark
and obdurate, stoic with years. He looked up
with emptied eyes as my shoes creaked the front step—
*here is what the dark brooms have swept away*—and not
until my voice was familiar in the air did he rise
from his chair and gesture me into his house.

# FIELD NUMEROLOGY

Nine crows in five days.
And if there are six snakes, and one

shucks its skin, becomes incorporeal,
is the sky still forever with birds,

these birds that map the grass
with their black stains?

And when the corn comes down,
four field mice enter the house

and hide behind the kitchen sink.
Then come winter, one horse dies

and waits for spring to be buried,
mounded in a lump of white.

It snows in our lungs, and driving
down the road we see the flakes

drifting like dust in air. Last
winter the bridge was out

for nineteen days, and the widower
who hanged himself

was spotted by seven children
on a school bus.

And then, this morning, there were
spots of blood on two eggs,

more beads sliding on
the imagined abacus.

Or now our monologue
of moonlight makes of the field

this arithmetic of grief. At dawn
we count three deer at the field's

edge, two fissures in the window
glass. And the crows count

slowly with each call: *one, two,*
*three, four, five.*

# CROW MUSIC

In Edvard Munch's
*Melancholy*, the sea sags

eternal tedium
to shore, and the man—

palm cupping chin—
gazes through half-drooped

lids to admit a meager
sliver of the world.

       *

My father would smoke
cigarettes on the porch

and call out to the crows,
single syllables in discrete

repeated units, sounds
like desultory drumbeats.

Itinerant dusk swelled
beyond the field,

inevitable with shadow,
and my father,

motionless, watched
the birds, immaculate

in grass, perfect black
obelisks, lifting

themselves as
extravagant darkness.

*

At his funeral
a lone

black feather
in the open

maw, crows
cawing in usable light,

the grammar
of desiccated grass,

an idolatry of mud
that makes a field,

my father
calling to birds

that were calling back,
saying nothing.

# ECONOMICS

*-Depression is rage spread thin.*

—George Santayana

It was a form of weakness, my father said,
an embarrassment, the men after the War
who were hollowed out, were grass
in the field behind the house, men who slept
amid the shadows of their days, who existed
like cigarette smoke—idle and drifting—
and shuddered at backfiring pickups and saw
their life's labor as a stroll to the mailbox
for the government check. When I was twelve,
my father returned from a trip to Chicago
with 500 off-brand batteries purchased
on the cheap from a company going out
of business, and so I was sent on my bicycle
to the farm houses and clusters of neighborhoods
in our small Ohio town. There was something
holy in labor, my father believed, but what I
remember is how discouraging it felt to ask
strangers again and again to reach into their pockets
for cash they didn't have. Sometimes the old
women or men who opened the doors
eyed me the way the moon eyes the earth,
the way the clouds are part of the sky
but also separate from it. Then, in college,
I worked one summer on mosquito abatement,
and my primary job was to step from the truck
to the road's verge and count how many
mosquitoes bit me in a minute. I was a poor
man's St. Francis of Assisi, but my father
was impressed by the work ethic evident in
the manifold bumps on my arms and legs,
impressed the way he never was with my meager
sales of the batteries that mostly still remained
in a cardboard box in his garage during the final

years of his life, when I would find him sitting
on the couch with the television blaring the same
cycle of news, over and over. There was a stillness
about him then, a smallness, as though the grass
had grown up around him in great, empty stalks.
The years and the sun had freckled his hands
with dark splotches, and often he seemed to be
studying their hieroglyphics, pondering what
the slow decades had wrought, and his unshaven
face was listless as the clouds. The days blurred
together after that, were like the fallen oak by
the fence, hollowed at the middle and spilling
its dark salt. My father had little, if anything,
to say, though he did tell me one early morning
that he imagined the advantage of being dead
was that the living would finally leave you be.

# Fourteen Omens in Nine Days

These grackles at dusk are telling a story of dark fire.
Then days pass and wraiths of sunlight ash the heart-ripe

hours, each breath a priest, the weeks as dim and constricted
as a pupil. Or a light rain drifts down, the odor of damp weeds,

the grackles now at first light a neurological firestorm.
Or we watch the solitary magnolia beside the garden, thorns

of brambles and dark dirt, or watch my father on the porch,
smoking, the ash on his cigarette lengthening but not yet falling.

He knows to enter a room inside himself, to close the door
and turn off the lights, to sit in the dark with his bourbon-colored

thoughts—until all we see is this vigil he keeps with himself,
the blue cigarette smoke almost too weary to lift into air.

# CODA

So now these flies making a helmet
on the skull of a dead raccoon

at the road's verge, this recurring
dream of years that fall away, the pearl

white moon with its barrenness
and beauty, that opens for us its manifold

arms, earth with its argument of mud,
loam bed carrying us forever,

sky garden and fertile stars so far away
we know they are a map. Or soon

the wind enclosing us in decades,
this long marriage of summer evenings

and flocks of birds, the birches
whispering of sacrifice and sorrow,

the grass a caress against our legs.
And suddenly the smell from the lowlands

of the first decay, primitive and ancient,
original death with its blackened trees

and drying rivers, nothing human here
except the surgery of hours, one slicing into

the body of the next, days of soot
and the quiet story of bootprints

in snow, a few frail years before
our lips are sewn tight and lamplight

grows so dull around us we sense
that we are drifting out to sea.

# NIGHT MUD

The belief that the moon
    was buried in the sky.
A fragment of bone, perhaps,
    or chipped stone. To understand
that what was visible was lost: a strange
    luminescence above the fields
at night, stars like frog eggs smearing
    above pitch pines. And the grave-
yard down the road alive with the dead,
    all of them crowding into
the earth. In my dreams there was
    blood on the snow in winter,
red smears by the swimming pool diving
    board where a boy slipped and fell,
blood on the bandages and above the ridge
    at dusk, the red blotches
on chests of soldiers in my father's
    Civil War book, the lost
limbs and the stumps of days.
    Then the calf that wouldn't
suckle and so died, and the mare
    my father dragged with his tractor
to be buried past the woods.
    Or once a mouse that succumbed
in our walls but couldn't be found,
    the smell of death bitter in the nostrils,
as though each body ripens and returns
    to the manure field, what clings
to the bottoms of your boots.

# WE KNOW THE GRASS

These old men have lived so long they believe in
the simplicity of snow: how it comes to you out of

your own body, arrives like a husk, like grass arching
its back in a wind. I see the men stamping their feet

and trying to keep warm, rubbing their fingers as they
stand by the river, which has crusted over with ice.

At night the men watch the moon make an augury
of smoke and sky. Their families worry how absent-

minded they've become, how they study the faint brush
strokes of morning, study the grackles becoming black streaks

of sky, lonely as blindfolds. Their wives grow impatient
with the years, blaming the snow or the grass or the blur

of the birds oaring toward them. But the old men can't
stop gazing at the river. They have questions they can't

answer, questions arranged like worn slacks folded at
the back of a chair, like grass brushing against your ankles

and legs. What remains is only this thin film of glaucoma
after dark where the moon moors in place amid the clouds,

this syringe of pale light pouring itself into the sky's flesh.

# FIELD GUIDE AT DUSK

It will not do. This weak-willed light slipping
from the grass, pale as hands folded on a chest.
No breeze to animate the hickory leaves,
to ripple the surface of the creek.
Just the fixed body of summer—the dimming
ghosts of the milkweeds and brambles,
tall as a boy's shoulder, tall as a man's waist.
Call it another covenant of evening: to feel the grass
unspool around us as we walk. To whisper
close against our bodies. This coven of bats
lifting in the evening air, as though pieces of the earth
have given way. The sound of the hinged wings
like a kind of short-sightedness: let the noise of it
carry across our field and no farther. This myopia
of evening: darkness gathering by our feet,
pooling around our legs, the world vanishing
from the bottom up. So much is lost like this.
To imagine our creek as a snake wending
through a field, creating this rut or runnel
as it muscles on its belly. This creek
and its fur of grass: some creature forming
itself from the night sky. To walk here
blindfolded by the darkness, until there is
only the grass against our bodies, the ghostly
hands of something springing from the earth.

# AFTER FOUR DAYS OF RAIN THE SKY FORGETS

The crows of childhood have arrived above the river,
landing in the field to dig up new shoots of corn,

perching as dark fire in the paper birches. As boys
we heard them calling out of their bodies, saw

their fallen feathers black as prophecy in the grass,
imagined their orange eyes watching my brother

rubbing salt into my ankles, the leeches that clung
there foaming blood then letting go. We are useless

in this: the birds slip in and out of years the way rain
drips without memory from the leaves. We slept

beneath stars, drifted in our father's rowboat in muddy
waters, floated on our backs and let the current

carry us. The crows rowed above my father wiping
his face with a handkerchief in the field, rowed above

my mother and aunt attaching a rope to a possum
skull so that it became a soundless wind chime

dangling from a hickory, rowed past the school bus
appearing at the fork in the road by the First Baptist

Church of Grace, rowed above the ambulance turning
one summer evening into the gravel drive, rowed

past the train tracks where the lovers parked their cars
and looked through windshields at a moon listing

placid and inhuman in a sky.

)  )

*MOON*

# OCTOBER MUD

For a long time the spirits thought they were
the alterations, the cadences. They lived in the ribs
of moonlight, in the robes of falling leaves. There was
a tapering wick of dusk behind my father's barn,
the field with its fragmentations of mud
and grass, the neighbor girl with her black horse
beyond the fence, the hoof prints and their pock-
marked hieroglyphics in hard dirt. All of this
was sensibility, uncultivated wraiths each time
I watched the distant light of her bedroom window,
the instep of moon above the trees. I pushed down
longing the way the flies sometimes clung
to the dead raccoon or possum at the road's verge,
or sometimes levitated above the open swales,
this decaying occultation, this manner
of whispering without making any sound.

# SACRED MUSIC

This wind—
wailing across

a carapace
of snow—

is bitter
and uncertain,

a small
god of gray light

weeping at
the edges

of railroad tracks,
gusts rattling

windows, cold air
seeping into

fissures,
like the sudden,

startled intake
of breath

I heard last
July when

a young girl,
perhaps fourteen,

dressed in summer
shorts, a T-shirt,

and flip-flops
stepped through

the wrong door
at the YMCA

and witnessed five
aging men—

none with towels,
our bodies primitive

with years, mud
thick around

our bellies, our
hair decaying gray

or white,
knobs between

our legs—
so fled,

or crows calling
in dark voices

from the yard
when my cousin—

both of us
not yet nine—

began thrashing
on the grass

with her first
seizure, as though

trying to free
herself from

the constraints
and burdens

of the body.

# ANCIENT BLIGHT

He imagines an antidote to birds, the sky

for once without the black stain. Morning

opens its shut lid. His wife, asleep,

dreams of different soil. Here are our

frenetic wings, our calls. Out the back door

the small compartments of leaves know nothing.

There is only fluttering, flittering. The sky

believes in gray inside of gray. The first birds

must have risen from the mud, carried

the dream of their contagion into air.

History is what overwhelms, invades.

He imagines a marriage being trapped

somehow in the birdlime of the moon,

the years of it thrashing into dark stars.

# MUD GRASS

She wanted a child. And so she waded
into the grass at twilight, grass the color

of a burnt biscuit, hip-tall, wild, damp
in the swales, smoke grass where she

and her lover spread the blanket by
the curvature of stream. Smears of starlings

oaring above shooting stars, rattlesnake master,
purple prairie clover. Birds skimming

low, an infection of wings and splotched
bodies. Here was the oracle of black stains

and their covenant with mud, the moon
a weed drifting above the creek that burrowed

forever into clay. The grass covered them
in bleary light—light like in Degas's *Bather*

*Drying Herself.* Pastel yellows, smudged oranges,
the body hidden the way grass unlimbs

itself in dirt and wind. This obsession
Degas had with women emerging from a bath,

faces subtracted. A vaginal dampness of grass,
whorls of it smearing and bending

by the creek. *Poa pratensis. Andropogon
scoparius.* Cloaking the lovers, sprawling,

grass like drawn shades, secret bodies.
Windfalls of earth, mud—grass trembling

and the sky hollow above. This lying
on the dirt beneath papered clouds,

beneath a gathering loam of night.

# Meditation and Form

A moon rises
inside this skull

of sky, the way a snake
can't decide

if it is paper skin
or living form.

And if the moon claims
the world as its first thought,

then the black water
of our bodies spreads

across the field
after so much rain,

full with thunderstorms
of temper and bad spirits.

Then a hoot owl's voice
presses through screen

mesh when I awake empty
in this bed. Surely our moon

is a wagon stalled
in a great prairie sea.

Surely it rolled out
from a thousand acres

of ribs and flesh,
to pause its ghostly heart

between beats.

# BLACK-SNAKE AUGURY

Everywhere there are omens:
hoot owls disentangling from gray bark,
dogwoods falling and spilling
their wood dust to stain the snow.
In July my mother drove us to Biloxi
and the Mississippi Sound, the heat
collecting its loam inside our lungs,
pressing its damp mouth against us.
I woke to a lone cockroach
on the bedroom ceiling, the creature
wanting nothing but to squeeze into
a tiny fissure where wall and ceiling
joined. I knew it was possible to live
like that, hours or weeks like a held
breath, secret years waiting out of sight.
My aunt asked me to help her outside
so she could show me an unripe pecan
on a tree in the backyard. Years later,
a colleague with pancreatic cancer described
his final weeks as sitting at an outdoor
café in April when the air is brisk enough
to make you ready to be gone from it, warm
enough to tempt you to stay. My aunt,
despite the southern sun, wore a sweater—
here is this skin of clothing we discard—
not unlike the paper skin I had thought
I was approaching on the deer path,
motionless as rope. Though when I reached
down, the creature roused itself
to lunge within inches of my hand.
There are signs everywhere—
crows calling from the distance, clouds
trailing their shadows, a black snake
muscling off into the grass.

# FIELD RELIGION

The old men fishing at the river
believe their hearts are bruised.
Or sometimes they imagine
a certain wildness inside their
chests, a cabal of grackles making
an augury of shrouded wings.
At night they watch the moon's
dull light—pale as insect larvae—
collecting on the skin of the earth.
The world becomes as illiterate
as loam. And this morning I watched
a turkey vulture pivot into its death
somersault—the passing pickup
clipped it as it lifted into air from
the red raw of a dead raccoon.
And years ago following an ice storm,
I saw another vulture perching
where a large limb of a hickory
had broken off overnight,
leaving a great open wound,
as though the bird had been
trapped inside for many decades,
believing it was bark or stone.
And what the bird said was *nothing*.
Or soon it will be winter and the old men
will stop fishing in the river past
our fence, will watch, from
their own windows, snow falling
on the nervous horses in the field.
Is this what the earth demands?
The men will realize, perhaps,
how death is consensual.
And after I saw the vulture
atop the severed tree, I learned
that the woman in the green
house down the road—
I knew her because our young

children were close friends—
had died the previous day of
breast cancer. In my dream
that night a hundred or a
thousand birds began fleeing
from the opening in
the hickory, somersaulting
across the air, until
everywhere was dark stain.

# Alluvial Prophecy

We see the old men from our windows,
fishing in the river. This must be the place
where sorrow goes, a penance of dark crows
flying out amid the trees. And soon it will be
winter, season of priestly winds, and the old
men will know the pilgrimage of hours.
Surely they dream of yellow grass in an open
field, grass like the beautiful uncut hair of the dead.
They suspect that the moon each night
is a solitary bird, its white feathers as still
as when the ship of earth is stalled.
And the moonlight on the river is a consolation,
a syringe filling the world with the coming cold.
It snows in the lungs, ice forming on the lips
with a strange opulence of forgetfulness,
the disappearing moon still exposing
its shoulder like a lullaby.

# DEPOSITION

Say two birds at dusk in an auburn sky.
But which is the augury of which? Or then
a cottonmouth slipping like ripe fruit into the reeds.
Our ribs feeling as hollow as a stream bed.
As though there is nothing else: just this excavated
dullness. The tongue and mouth like small,
decaying animals. And the birds, no longer
in their bodies in the darkness, filling the air
with cries that ripple like small waves along
a water's surface, a last breath. *We formed*
*ourselves from mud and blood and spittle. From an old*
*ceiling of sky.* The broken spine of ridge coupling
with swollen clouds. The bitternut hickory shedding
its sorcery of leaves into the stream. And so the stars
bobbing like body parts amid a dim ocean of clouds.
Until there is nothing left, not even the birds
darting through the air like dreams. You sleepwalk
into it. The moon sealing itself to the lip of the earth.

*CROW*

# CROW NAMES

After we tired of words
    there was dark and darker.

A fine warm rain fell.
    You could hear them

beyond the gabled
    roofs, beyond the open

fields in the swales. Dusk
    became ash. No one

tended to the cries and they grew
    louder, claiming the back

roads past the railroad tracks,
    the bar ditches, rising

from pokeweed, leatherleaf.
    Pressing through

screen mesh, clinging to our clothes,
    following us down hallways.

We gave names to this:
    *disfigured creature, black moon,*

*shape of mind.* The sounds
    were stone and flesh, wound

and feathers. Circling
    the yards then circling

back. Carrying the stink
    of wet compost, loam rain.

Calling and calling
    to our scavenged bodies.

# BIRTH SONG

At dawn these birds are blackish
    and tangential, and the light
comes in low from the field,

unfathomable. There is a song
    the grass sings by holding still,
that my wife sings by leaning

against the window sill, her arms
    crossed and occasional:
*Here is the day that hasn't yet begun,*

*that holds itself for this moment*
    *in abeyance.* My neighbor
describes how when her child was born

not alive she held him the way
    a pond bed holds its stagnant
waters, how everything becomes

a form of statuary: to close your
    eyes and to feel the length
of a held breath, that sense

that our lives are the space
    between our heartbeats,
the instant before the eye blinks.

She dreams sometimes that her child
    begins squirming in her arms,
that the doctors begin hovering around her,

stunned by their mistake,
    and there is a moment
inside that dream when they are too

perplexed to rend the child
    from her arms to tend to him,
when she herself has not yet

come awake, an instant when the boy
    begins to open his mouth
to cry his way into the world.

# MUTE CLARINET

And above the field, a crow, shadowless, crossing
the winter grass, crossing the pale skin of snow

that must seem, from that height, like something
insubstantial—a few bright afterthoughts or patches

at the road's verge, where there are many crows
dipping with their black velocities. Or somehow

it is night and the granular stars are drifting unmoored
in the sky's mud. And always this impulse to glance up,

as though it is a way of conjuring the world, creating it
from a body not our own. Or imagine an old man's wife,

no longer living, who played the clarinet in high school,
and afterwards, after she marched her last occasion

with the band, kept the instrument in a dusty cardboard
box for many decades: mouthpiece, cap, ligature, barrel,

first joint, second, bell. And now how the horseweed
is a shadow beyond the barn where the woman's husband

is walking at first light, and he hears the bellows of wind
splintering the field where, in summer, the soybeans

yellow. For here is the naming of a thing, a languaging—
the conjured grass in the field beyond the fence,

remembered dandelions and milkweed shadowing mud,
sky and field smudging one against the other, blurring

the way the hours blur. For always, year round, the grass
is lonely, here at this place where the mud is anatomical,

this usury of minutes and the slaughter of hours.
And here, in winter, is the worded shivering of dead grass

spreading out before him, crows making sounds
that no one would ever mistake for music, but still

he names them spreading outward from the fallen
willow at the field's verge—these crows collecting

gray air, stoking a glowing coal of day with black wings.

# ORIGINAL EARTH

The winter my father became
a crow, he must have flown
out of the green ash, joining

the birds filling the field's
quadrant of dull sky. Then later
he called from the woods—

something deep at the bottom
of a well, a black crack where light
was too timid to venture.

# UNTITLED ORACLE

Our mothers are dust
on a windowsill,
a divination of milkweed.

And these old men
in their rowboats are fishing—
smoke in the eyes of years.

Or say the men drowned
once in marsh marigold,
the unending

stillness of cattails
and calamus. A lone
white cloud drifted

by slowly as a hearse.
A sinew of night
and the head aches.

And if we are a black
wagon dragged by
a black horse, we trade

mythologies for another
cup of coffee. Someone
loves us like a moth

against a lamp.
And when we wake,
there are unexceptional

yellow jackets on fallen
apples, August skies, cloud
cataracts, mists of rain.

# MEASURE

Plato believed all love is the desire for immortality.
And earlier tonight when we watched a ringneck snake

emerging from the tall grass, we saw its lateral undulations,
its concertina locomotions. And above us, birds were

rowing their dark boats, and night was beginning to form
in the clay of sky. It is too easy to imagine the years

as windswept inside our chests, the hours vanishing. And if
last year a fire claimed the hickories beyond the railroad

tracks, cleaving to the earth, rising out of the lungs
of August, now the partridge pea flowers are spreading out

from the deer path where night is crowding beside the creek.
Later, perhaps, we will carry a blanket into the grass

where moonlight will spill its wild measure. Bodies know
to interrogate the wheel of earth. Your face, beneath mine,

will follow the contours of the clouds. And when stars bloom
beyond our sight, we will sense the palpitations of the grass.

And if we dream tonight that willow polypores are springing
from our skin, that we are yoked to the rich smells of loam

across the bottomlands, slave to the geese passing overhead
on their grooves of air, surely the moon will remain devout

above us. *Come quietly*, it will whisper. And if our hearts
are instruments, if we are drunk with this unknowing, here

are the shadows where lovers lie down in summer grass,
where wind ripples each stalk into prophecy and prayer.

# DREAM SKIN

The lovers have skinned their own bodies,
  are decaying in the woods.

They dream this the way a snake dreams
  the grass trembling when it muscles past.

 In the dream the snake has lost its own skin
  beside the river, or the river has lost

its own skin and is hardened mud. There are cracks
  in the mud that must be the fissures

of an ancient face. The lovers have swept out
  their house so that dust drifts

in a leisurely fashion toward the river,
  hangs in the air as though from

an invisible noose. The lovers know it is the daily
  rituals that last: to watch the shadows

falling against the sweetbay trees, staining
  the trunks. To walk down to the mailbox

and see the dandelions becoming ghosts.
  Sometimes they sense the openness

of their bodies, the way the skin of a snake believes
  that what is left behind is still a life.

# THE ARTIST'S ROOM

No one was there to see
    what happened,
and yet we inherited the deer path

through the woods, narrow
    and twisting, the way
the leaves catch the light and darken it,

so that the undersides are almost
    luminescent. And earlier
the turkey buzzards were circling

overhead, arising out of the slowness
    of the earth, and none
of us were there to witness

what was lost, all the years lifting
    out of the grass, the sound
of something moving through

the undergrowth, ghosts so frail
    they were little more than wind.
We never saw them nor could:

not the hazel alder growing out
    of the mud, lifting its arms
in defiance or maybe supplication,

the stream that dried in August
    then swelled in June,
without wanting, the moon

with its scarred and lonely face.
    So many years
sleeping so never noticing,

without a thought or dream,
        just the deer
moving sometimes at dawn

or dusk, their bodies brushing
        the tall grass on either side
of the path,

so that the stalks trembled
        for a moment
before growing still.

# CROW EPISTLES

My father flew away finally
with the crows. And then it was winter.

We heard him calling sometimes
from the woods as snow came down.

It was a kind of faith, the falling snow.
And always the crows seemed harmless

in the trees. The hours were blind
beyond the river, an offering

of masked leaves and broken earth,
the wet smell of mud in the swales,

snow prints in our dreams that arced
down to the river then back,

approaching the back door
like tooth marks in an apple.

And once we saw a lone black feather
dropped and resting in the falling

snow, snow that wanted nothing
from the field but its erasure.

And come morning the crows
were gathering in the distance,

watching the snow coming down,
the obelisks of their black bodies

motionless, the way you might
imagine a prayer arising

from the stillness of a breath.
Though later, after dark, the nightly

drama of the moon conducted
its pale sojourn above the trees,

where it briefly stayed before
drifting its smoke toward the river.

*TONGUE*

# The Human Velocity

When, last August, our neighbor's house burned down,
and smoke drifted its dark figure to suffocate the line

of field where the river bent between our houses,
it was easy to imagine deer watching ghostly

from the tree line, mud watching from the tufts
of grass, the sky watching from its inhuman distance.

Here was the makeshift body, the loam and sluggish
current of our lives, a blossoming like birds collecting

their dim gray in a dusk sky. And since we live in a circuitry
of shadows, in mud and the black cloth of the river

after dark, in these burning days of summer, we have
nothing more to call ourselves, no name sounding right

on the tongue, the moon a mute reliquary above our houses,
the grass asleep beneath the half-blind stars. Our neighbors

stayed with us for two weeks, and from our back windows
they could hear the birds calling from the willows,

could see the skeletal remains across the river.
It is easy to grow afraid of the sky, its eyelid

with its darkening ink. And when, come winter, snow
falls out of it, snow and its layers of pale linen,

we imagine this as the mute tongue enclosed in
its tomb of hardened mud. Sometimes, I know,

my neighbors heard the wind speaking against
their back screen door spared by the flames,

sounding like something living clawing for
a last breath—the way an owl calls from its high tree,

feeling the wind roaring from the fields.

# DARKENED AND FORGETFUL

This grass is forgetful beyond the fence,
      and made of angels that masquerade

as grackles. And east of the railroad tracks,
      behind brick walls of a farmhouse built

long before anyone alive was ever born,
      our neighbor woman is counting down

her last breaths, the way these crows stir
      dimming air into a frenzy. And down here,

down in the lowlands where mosquitoes are
      made of mud and loam of flesh, I swing

this scythe against weeds and towering grass,
      a small death assignable to nothing,

our moon kneeling between the river birches.
      While our neighbor, I've been told,

reels her last breaths to shore,
      and the grackles, untouchable beyond

the fence, are black and becoming blacker—
      drifting soot from a great and distant fire.

# UNTITLED LOVE

Or say we made ashes of this bed.

The way it feels
to stand at a window and watch

the streets and sidewalks
gathering snow,
hoarding it,

some unknown wing fluttering
in our chests,

something untitled evolving out
of the quiet, emerging from
this hospice

of desire—this skinned fish
thrown back into the waves

before it knows that it has died.

# FOUR DANCERS

I believe last winter wasn't a crossroads after all,
no than more than this fallen river birch lying half

in the moving stream and half on the bank—
inert in quiet sunlight—is a choice. I choose

the sound of wind across snow-covered fields,
a neighbor's abandoned barn with its great rifts

opening to the sky. As a child I dragged bluegills
from my father's pond, fish that used their sharp

fins to draw blood from my palms, the brightness
dripping into the shallows and becoming real.

Now my friend, dying of brain cancer, claims
his memories press like bone through skin,

and I recall Degas's four dancers with red
lips and red straps on pale shoulders,

dancers with arms raised, twirling in open
air before sky and greenery, though of course

they aren't truly moving after all but are
stationary, the way a child dangles his legs

from a dock into a pond, watching shadows
of fish slipping always in and out of existence.

# CHRONIC OFFERINGS

To the gods we give the cold sky,
these meager flares of stars, magic
hair of midnight when we sleep,
entrails of dreams. Ice hardens along
the body of the earth, my father with
his homesickness for death, my mother
with the distance between garden
and sky, birds loud at dusk
each time my wife crosses her legs
at the ankles and evening plumes
then drifts then disappears. We offer
summer heat, taillights of memories,
whir of cicadas beyond the fence,
children running by the river
with darkened feet, alarms of desperation
when loved ones die, live on
without us, our tongues broken
at the root, the years undressing
then leaving us, this waiting on the sofa,
our feet up, or walking in the field
where caretaker grass grieves
and swirls around our legs, the clouds
a gray current, our endless passages
of recriminations and regrets, the love
we felt once like a bird speeding toward
the bright light of a window.

# First Winter

And if when we die we set fire to the fields of our memories,
our skin coming loose the way dusk sky peels bright

along its edges, if mud dreams us and yet there are gates
opening and closing, rumors of the loneliness of moonlight,

myths of existing through the centuries without knowing
what's been lost, strangers to the lanterns that once

guided us, blind as fever, must we still dress ourselves
from time to time in these old clothes, rise like mist above

the stone fence, move out across the human cold?

# ONCE MORE NAMING THE CROWS

In the high grass the shadows forget.
      It has come to this: morning
cold and nothing else. Just the testimonials
      of wind and the puckered clouds
that want nothing then retreat. It is how
      to make a distance of a thing: to imagine
the closed doorways and dark mornings
      as suitors of each other, the old lovers
of snow falling and clinging, describing
      an open field. Or then the living mud
that hardens the way the widower hardens
      himself in the back yard while chopping
wood, then returns to the house to pour
      himself a cup of coffee. By day the moon
forgets that there's a sky, can't imagine
      what it means to hang suspended there,
and the man remembers his wife's name
      as something slipping from a body,
holding itself aloft above a field in gray light,
      unmoored and drifting, moving through
the snow with the nameless crows that gather
      amid the harvested corn. He believes
he is undone in this, has chosen the dark
      figures in the orderly stubble,
as though to form a name too often
      on the lips is to make it disappear.

# CROW SYMPHONY

In the end, a single black feather
is visible at noon in open mud.

It seems a storm is coming, the hours
half-buried in shadow. And my father,

because he is waiting past the trees, because
I close my eyes to the dark mirror,

is lost to us in this prayer of crows.
The bloody berries drooping on the vine.

The small circle of tree stumps where the field
begins. Or now the symphony of wind,

the filigreed clouds explosive
above the railroad tracks, swirling.

Crow memories and crow cries
like heavy stones, the black coat of night

where the hours open to my father's white
pills on the nightstand, the empty bottles

by the dresser. This reunion of memories
becoming a language of continuance,

what joins or falls or wakes me in the morning—
the black trumpets of a dream. And here,

by the fence, the bodies of the horses
heavy in summer air, the smell

like steeped sunlight. Or my father's
childhood in Michigan—the rooming house,

his grandmother's whispering, the Depression
a leaky valve. The days carved by the lake

to become this dreamscape of forgetting.
Formed from clay, molded by unseen hands,

heated in the kiln of decades. To focus
on a crow feather staining the mud,

mud that in January was covered by snow,
the dark earth invisible beneath it.

To sleep and wake—to be ritualized by wonder.
This storm that is formless in the trees, black

against black where the horses edge
nearer to the fence, close as a warm breath.

And now this fervor of rain coming down,
claiming everything it touches as its own.

## Acknowledgments

Grateful acknowledgment is made to the editors of the following publications where poems in this collection, sometimes in slightly different forms, were originally published:

*AGNI*: "Coda," "Crow Epistles," and "Meditation and Form"

*Alaska Quarterly Review*: "Darkened and Forgetful," "Dream Skin," "First Winter," and "Night Mud"

*American Literary Review*: "Alluvial Prophecy"

*Arts & Letters*: "Once More Naming the Crows"

*Carolina Quarterly*: "Field Religion"

*The Fiddlehead* (Canada): "Mud Grass"

*The Georgia Review*: "Crow Music"

*Green Mountains Review*: "Crow Symphony" and "Sacred Music"

*The Greensboro Review*: "Mute Clarinet" and "October Mud"

*Hunger Mountain*: "Field Guide at Dusk" and "Deposition"

*The Los Angeles Review*: "Ancient Blight" and "Crow, Moon, Crow"

*Meridian*: "Untitled Love"

*Natural Bridge*: "Four Dancers," and "Untitled Oracle"

*The New York Quarterly*: "The Artist's Room"

*Prairie Schooner*: "After Four Days of Rain the Sky Forgets," "Crow Names," and "Birth Song"

*Slate*: "Life in the Woods"

*The South Carolina Review*: "Economics," "The Human Velocity," "Measure," "Original Earth," and "We Know the Grass"

*Southern Humanities Review*: "Chronic Offerings"

*The Southern Review*: "Black-Snake Augury"

*storySouth*: "Field Numerology"

*Valparaiso Poetry Review*: "Fourteen Omens in Nine Days"

The Michael Waters Poetry Prize was established in 2013 to honor Michael's contributions to *Southern Indiana Review* and American arts and letters.

Inaugural Prize-winner Doug Ramspeck is the author of four previous poetry collections. His most recent book, *Mechanical Fireflies* (2011), received the Barrow Street Press Poetry Prize. His first book, *Black Tupelo Country* (BkMk Press, 2008), received the John Ciardi Prize for Poetry. His poems have appeared in journals that include *Slate*, *The Kenyon Review*, *The Georgia Review*, *Alaska Quarterly Review*, and *AGNI*. Ramspeck is an associate professor at The Ohio State University at Lima, where he teaches creative writing and directs the Writing Center.

Michael Waters has written ten books of poetry, including *Gospel Night* (2011); *Darling Vulgarity*, finalist for the *Los Angeles Times* Book Prize (2006); and *Parthenopi: New and Selected Poems*, finalist for the Paterson Poetry Prize (2001). His poems have appeared in various journals, including *The Yale Review*, *The Paris Review*, *The Kenyon Review*, *Poetry*, *The Georgia Review*, and *Rolling Stone*. Among his awards are fellowships from the National Endowment for the Arts and the Fulbright Foundation and fellowship residencies at Yaddo, MacDowell, The Tyrone Guthrie Center (Ireland), Le Chateau de Lavigny (Switzerland), and The St. James Centre for Creativity (Malta). He is a professor of English at Monmouth University and also teaches in the Drew University MFA Program in Poetry and Poetry in Translation. Waters lives with his wife, poet Mihaela Moscaliuc, in Ocean, New Jersey.

# Books by Doug Ramspeck

*Mechanical Fireflies*
*Possum Nocturne*
*Where We Come From*
*Black Tupelo Country*